Turret clock, 1386

Gothic alarm clock, 1450

3rd lamp clock, 1550

Drum clock, 1560

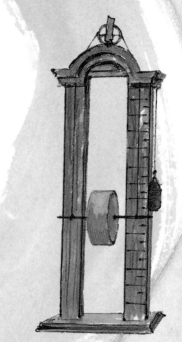

Clock watch, 1590

Through the Ages

Water-drum clock, 1605

Bracket clock, 1750

Watch, 1697

Table clock, 1610

American long-case clock, 1795

About TIME

About TIME

A FIRST LOOK AT TIME AND CLOCKS

By Bruce Koscielniak

Houghton Mifflin Company Boston 2004

www.houghtonmifflinbooks.com

The text of this book is set in 14-point Sabon.
The illustrations are watercolor.

ISBN-13: 978-0-618-39668-9
ISBN-10: 0-618-39668-3

Library of Congress Cataloging-in-Publication Data
Koscielniak, Bruce.
About time : a first look at time and clocks/ by
Bruce Koscielniak.
p. cm.
Summary: Describes the concept of time and how it has been
measured throughout history, using water clocks, sundials,
calendars, and atomic vibrations.
ISBN 0-618-39668-3
1. Time—Juvenile literature. 2. Time measurements—Juvenile
literature. [1. Time. 2. Time measurements.] I. Title.
QB209.5.K67 2004
529.7—dc22
2003017469
Printed in Singapore
TWP 10 9 8 7 6 5 4 3 2 1

For Fran and the gift antique clock

Time.

Time to read a book.
Time to wash dishes.
Time to do this or that.

We look at the clock and know that we have five minutes more to sleep, or to catch the bus. We know that things called events happen as those minutes tick by.

And when the clock has moved ahead by, say, five minutes, we know that "time" has passed, because the events of those minutes are now just a memory.

Simple enough. The clock sweeps ahead, and everything left behind tumbles down a drainpipe from the here-and-now into some mysterious place called "the past."

Well, maybe it's not all so simple, but let's take a closer look at this idea we all must live with—time.

Time waits for no one.
Time flies.
Time is on my side.

We've all probably heard some version of the many old sayings about time that abound, and that's because it's a topic people frequently think about. No surprise there.

Time for most of us is the organizing principle in our daily lives, and its passage sweeps us all from cradle to grave. It's not really possible to ignore time or its effects on us.

So how do we define "time"?

We can begin by saying that time is what is measured by a regular or standard interval—a second, a minute, an hour, for example—that is chimed, ticked, beeped, or in some way displayed by a time-measuring device called a clock. And people have always used some kind of clock.

Our ancient ancestors relied on the sun for daily timekeeping. For them it was either "nighttime" or "daytime," and when the sun was directly overhead, it was "midday"—our noontime.

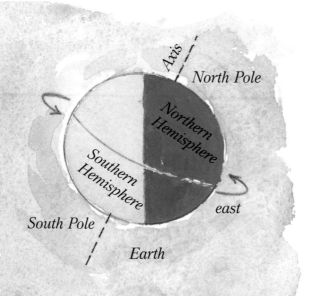

Axis

North Pole

Northern Hemisphere

Southern Hemisphere

east

South Pole

Sun

Earth

The day

Each day (a twenty-four-hour period) the earth makes one complete spin or "rotation" on its axis, an imaginary center spindle running through the North and South Poles. The earth's eastward spin brings about day and night.

Seasonal time—the coming of winter, the return to spring and summer—was of particular importance for survival, and this could be determined by noting moon cycles and the seasonal position of the sun in the sky.

Third quarter

The month
The moon completes a revolution around the earth every month (29 ½ days).

Sun

Earth

New moon

Full moon

Moon's orbit

First quarter

Equinox means equal length of night and day.

North Pole

Vernal equinox March 21

WINTER

SPRING

South Pole

N

Winter

The axis tilting toward the sun brings summer in the Northern Hemisphere.

Sun

Winter solstice December 21

Summer

N

S

Summer solstice June 21

S

The axis tilts away, causing winter in the Southern Hemisphere.

N

AUTUMN

SUMMER

Autumnal equinox September 21

S

Earth's orbit

The year
Each year (365 ¼ days) the earth completes a revolution around the sun, causing the seasons. Because the earth's axis is tilted, the hemisphere tilted toward the sun is warmer, the hemisphere tilted away is cooler.

As people kept records of the natural divisions of time—days, moon cycle months, yearly cycles of the seasons—they were able to predict the coming season and know with some accuracy how many days of warm, cool, or rainy weather they would have. These records were called calendars.

Around 3500 B.C., the Sumerians, probably the first people to widely use a calendar, had a lunar-based (or moon-based) year of twelve months (new moon cycles) made up of thirty days each.

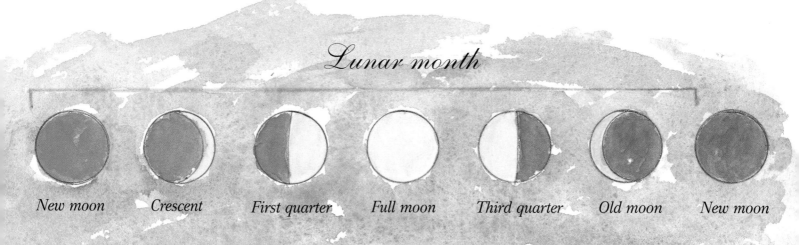

Lunar month

| New moon | Crescent | First quarter | Full moon | Third quarter | Old moon | New moon |

Phases of the moon as seen from Earth

The Egyptians by 2600 B.C. had a solar-based (or sun-based) calendar of 365 days, and they began their year with the rising in the east of Sirius, the "Dog Star," which coincided with the flooding of the Nile.

The "week," which is not a natural division of time, has had to be set by each society—days for work, worship, rest. The Greeks used three ten-day weeks per month. The Romans used an eight-day week with the eighth day reserved for market festivities, but after A.D. 200 they changed to a seven-day week.

The difficulty in making a calendar, however, is that natural time cycles do not fit neatly together into yearly units. A year—that is, one full revolution of the earth around the sun—is longer than twelve new moon cycles and contains a fraction more than 365 days. Therefore, days must be added to keep the calendar in time with the actual seasons.

The Roman ruler Julius Caesar in 46 B.C. put together a 365-day calendar based on the Egyptian model but beginning the year on January 1, and he ordered that every fourth year an extra day be added to the month of February. This "leap year," however, over time, made the calendar run out of step with the seasons.

January 31 days	February 28 days + 1 every 4 years*	March 31 days	April 30 days
May 31 days	June 30 days	July 31 days	August 31 days
September 30 days	October 31 days	November 30 days	December 31 days

Gregorian Calendar

* except no leap year for the years 2100, 2200, 2300

In 1582, Pope Gregory XIII revised the "Julian" calendar by omitting three leap years every four centuries. That brought the calendar into close agreement with the actual seasons, and today we and much of the world continue to use the "Gregorian" calendar.

For daily timekeeping, a sundial consisting of an upright stick in the ground with time marks around it came into use around 3500 B.C. in early cities of Mesopotamia. And by 1500 B.C., in Egypt, the sticks were replaced with monumental decorated spires called obelisks, which were built in city centers.

THOTH

Stylus to record names

Symbol of life

The tops of obelisks were covered with gold to reflect the sun, particularly at the hours of sunrise and sunset.

Egyptians believed that Thoth, the god of time measurement, would weigh souls and make judgments about which ones were to live in the timeless afterworld.

S   W
E   N

For morning, the T faced east. In the afternoon, the sundial was turned and the T faced west.

The Egyptian ruler Thutmose III used a small, portable, T-bar sundial that cast a shadow over the time marks on its lower bar. This device, however, didn't work for the earliest and latest hours of daylight.

A more accurate sundial from 300 B.C., known as the hemicycle, was a stone half bowl with a metal pointer called a "gnomon", from the Greek "one who knows," which would cast its shadow on lines indicating the twelve daylight hours.

The Egyptians, Greeks, and Romans all divided the day and the night each into twelve equal parts called "hours." Hour means "one-twelfth part." Because the length of day and night are varied, so too the hours were of flexible length.

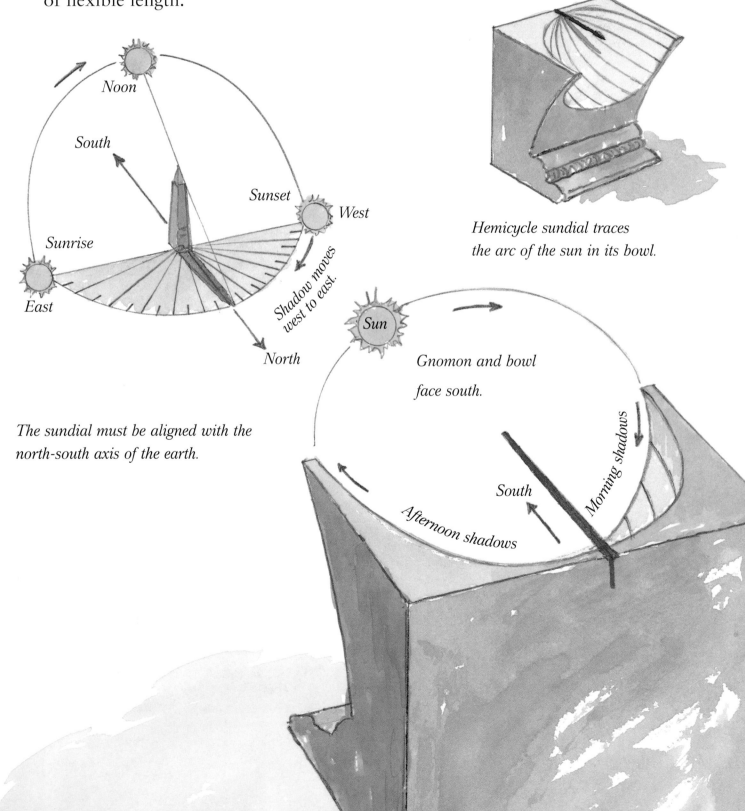

Hemicycle sundial traces the arc of the sun in its bowl.

The sundial must be aligned with the north-south axis of the earth.

Shadow moves west to east.

Gnomon and bowl face south.

Morning shadows

Afternoon shadows

Water clocks were devised to keep time at night or on cloudy days. First used in Egypt around 1380 B.C., an outflow water clock consisted simply of a large pot with a spout at the bottom that dripped water at a consistent rate. Measuring marks in the vessel would indicate how much time had passed based on the amount of water that had escaped. A second vessel could be attached to catch and reuse the water.

The Greeks and Romans employed water clocks and called them "clepsydra" or "thieves of water."

A more complicated inflow water clock was invented in 250 B.C., using a stream of water to raise a float with an "angel" figure that pointed to the time on a tall cylinder.

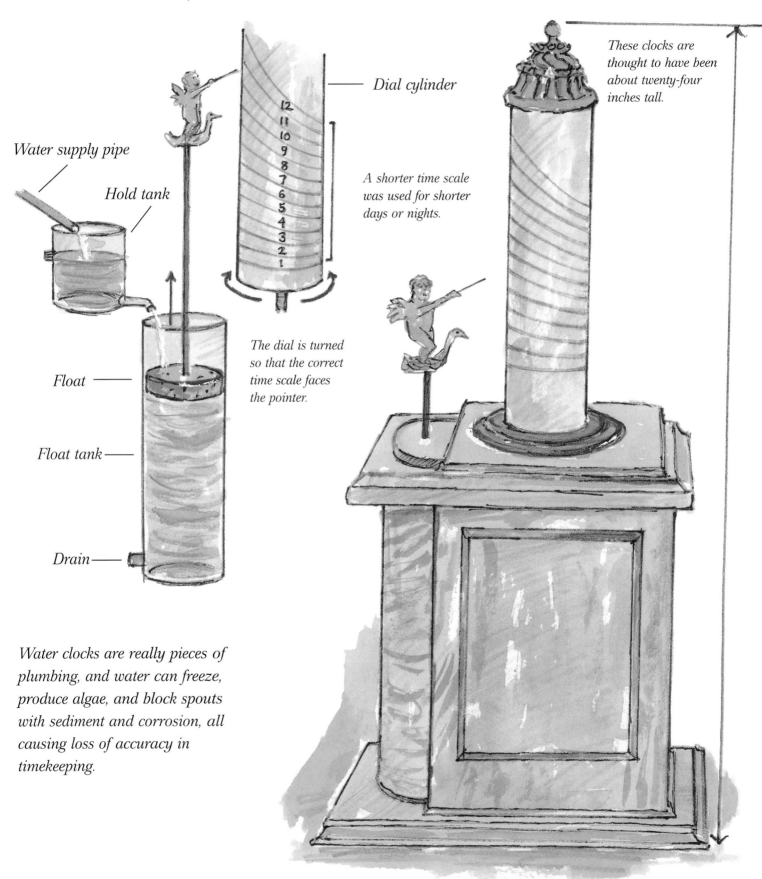

Water supply pipe

Hold tank

Float

Float tank

Drain

Dial cylinder

12
11
10
9
8
7
6
5
4
3
2
1

A shorter time scale was used for shorter days or nights.

The dial is turned so that the correct time scale faces the pointer.

These clocks are thought to have been about twenty-four inches tall.

Water clocks are really pieces of plumbing, and water can freeze, produce algae, and block spouts with sediment and corrosion, all causing loss of accuracy in timekeeping.

Over the centuries, in China and the Middle East, water clocks became elaborate mechanisms, such as the large water-wheel clock made by the Chinese builder Su Sung around A.D. 1088, which included quarter-hour gongs and moving time-telling and astronomical figures.

Armillary showing positions of planets and stars. Painted time-telling figures turn on large wheels.

In China, emperors built grand astronomical clocks to show that they were connected with the heavens—and for practical use. This clock had a stop-and-go movement—while the water bucket filled, the clock stopped. When the bucket was full, the weight of the water tripped a lever to allow the clock to turn one notch.

Water bucket

Water supply

Medieval monasteries in Europe used water clocks with bells to strike devotional, work, and dining hours. The science of timekeeping is called horology, and a clock of the Middle Ages was referred to as the horologium.

Monastic water wheel, bell clock of the thirteenth century

Hourglass sand clock

Candle clock

Oil lamp clock

Candle clocks and lamp clocks were also used in the Middle Ages. It took a certain amount of time for a candle or oil lamp to burn from one mark to the next.

As glass-making techniques developed in Europe, sand-pouring clocks kept time. In use from about A.D. 1200 until after 1600, hourglass clocks poured sand from an upper glass bulb into another lower one, through a tiny hole at the narrow center. When all the sand had poured into the lower chamber, the clock was turned upside down to pour again.

European monasteries used seven
canonical (church) hours:

Matins/Lauds: First light
Prime: Sunrise
Tertia: Midmorning
Meridies: Noon
Nona: Midafternoon
Vespers: Sunset
Compline: Nightfall

But around A.D. 1275 in Europe something new was up and running. Someone, probably at a monastery in Burgundy, France, had invented the all-mechanical clock.

These first, rudimentary mechanical clocks consisted of iron gears set in an upright frame, and were powered by the pull of weights hanging on a rope wound around a wooden spindle, or barrel, attached to the drive wheel.

The clocks had no dials, only a bell struck by a hammer that would wake or alert a timekeeper, who then rang a large chapel bell to wake the other monks living in a monastery for prayer and work. This clock was an early version of the fully mechanical alarm clock!

Clock dials were introduced in Italy around 1344. Clocks at that time had only an hour hand, and Roman numerals were used because most people were not yet familiar with Arabic numbers.

1440 BELL CLOCK

Bell

Pedestal

Weight

Weight

Though early turret clocks had no time-telling dials, they often employed wood or metal figures called "jacquemart", or "jacks," to strike the bells and provide an entertainment each hour for the townspeople.

By 1335, mechanical bell clocks, striking twenty-four equal-length hours, had become monumental structures powered by massive weights and were built into chapel towers, or turrets, in towns and cities across Europe.

People woke, ate, prayed, and worked by the clock bells.

The word "clock" itself probably comes from the German word *Glocke,* meaning "bell." The public clock served to unite the town or city.

It is the invention of the "escapement" that made mechanical clocks possible. The escapement is so called because it allows the pull of the weight to "escape" through a check and release system—by one gear tooth at a time.

The first all-mechanical clocks used a T-shaped escapement called a "verge and foliot."

This simple device consisted of a rotating upright bar, the verge, having two flags, or pallets, that alternate to stop the crown wheel, which resembled a king's crown, and a shorter crossbar called the foliot, having weights at each end to regulate the speed at which the pallets engaged the crown wheel.

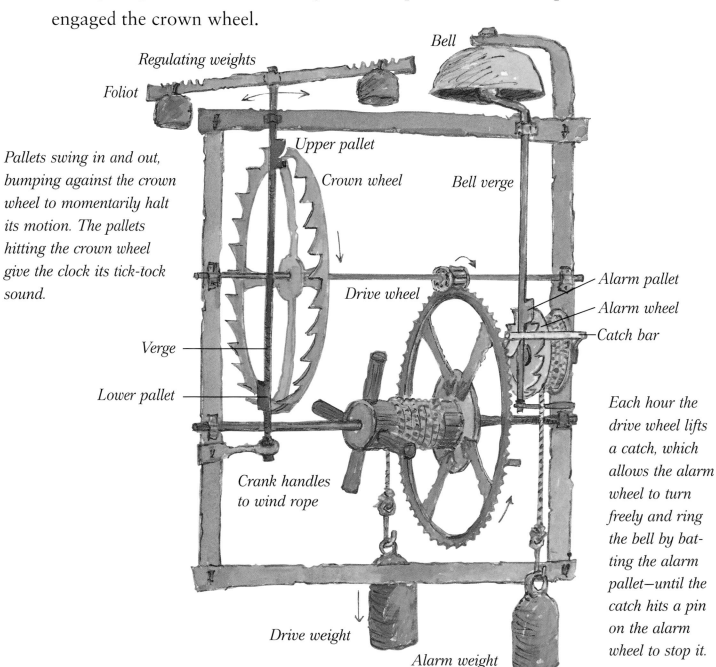

Regulating weights

Foliot

Bell

Upper pallet

Crown wheel

Bell verge

Pallets swing in and out, bumping against the crown wheel to momentarily halt its motion. The pallets hitting the crown wheel give the clock its tick-tock sound.

Drive wheel

Alarm pallet

Alarm wheel

Catch bar

Verge

Lower pallet

Crank handles to wind rope

Each hour the drive wheel lifts a catch, which allows the alarm wheel to turn freely and ring the bell by batting the alarm pallet—until the catch hits a pin on the alarm wheel to stop it.

Drive weight

Alarm weight

Sometime around 1440, the spring-powered clock was invented. Instead of depending on the pull of weights for power, this type of clock used a flat metal spring wound tightly into a coil. The escapement allowed the spring to unwind by turning one gear tooth at a time. With the use of a spring, smaller, truly portable clocks could be made.

The first well-known watches, made in Germany around 1510 by Peter Henlein, were so named because guards or "watchmen" carried small clocks to keep track of how long to stay at a particular duty post.

1599 SPRING WATCH

Early spring clocks were often drum-shaped, with the dial on top.

Spring

Crown wheel

1525 DRUM CLOCK

Many different skills went into making a clock, and new tools and methods were constantly being invented to make ever smaller, more complicated mechanisms that worked with greater precision.

Founders melted and poured metal into a mold to make clock parts.

Spring makers hand-forged (heated and pounded into shape) and polished steel clock springs.

Screw makers cut screws used to fasten clocks together by using a small lathe devised by a German clockmaker in 1480. Earlier, only wedges or pegs were used.

Gear-tooth cutting had been done by hand until the mid-1500s, when Giannelo Torriano of Cremona, Italy, invented a machine that could cut perfect gear teeth. Brass replaced iron for clock making.

Engravers, gilders, and enamelers decorated clock cases and dials.

Glass-making shops made and cut glass.

Woodworkers made clock cases.

In 1657, the Dutch mathematician Christian Huygens built a clock with a pendulum (instead of a foliot) to regulate the escapement, which did much to improve timekeeping precision. A minute hand was now routinely added to the hour hand on clock dials.

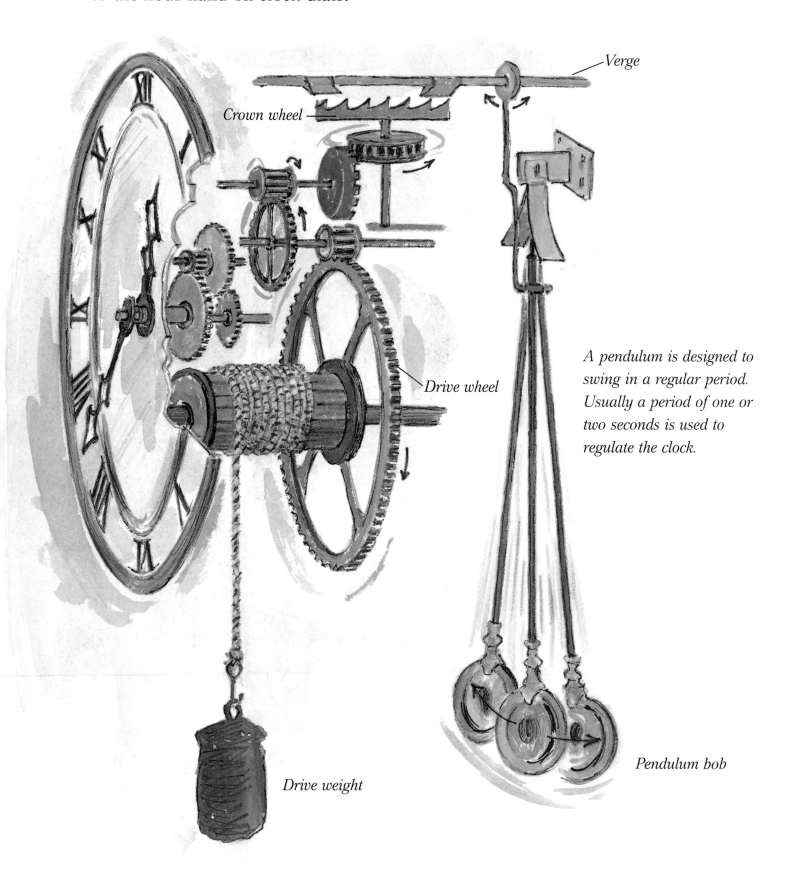

Verge

Crown wheel

Drive wheel

A pendulum is designed to swing in a regular period. Usually a period of one or two seconds is used to regulate the clock.

Pendulum bob

Drive weight

Balance wheel

Balance spring

Pallet

The balance spring rotates back and forth to swing the verge and pallets.

Crown wheel

Verge

Pallet

Twenty years after applying the pendulum to upright clocks, Huygens invented a new device called the balance spring, which could be used to regulate the verge in watches and portable clocks more accurately.

Today, clocks and watches use highly accurate mechanisms—some old, some new. In addition to weight-and spring-powered clocks, we now use electric clocks, in which electric current in various ways moves the dial display.

The first electric clock was a battery type invented in England in the early 1840s.

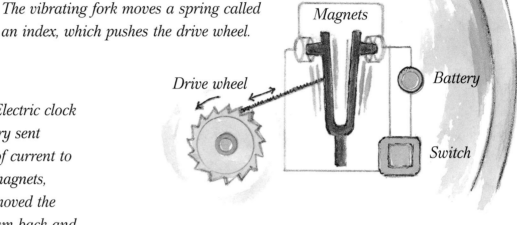

The vibrating fork moves a spring called an index, which pushes the drive wheel.

Magnets

Drive wheel

Battery

Switch

*1850 Electric clock
A battery sent pulses of current to electromagnets, which moved the pendulum back and forth to power the clock.*

*1960 Battery tuning fork watch
The battery makes the fork vibrate with a regular pulse.*

*Electric-motor clock
A small motor turns gears to move the clock hands.*

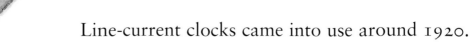

Line-current clocks came into use around 1920.

Quartz clocks and watches, developed in 1929, use a small battery to make a piece of quartz crystal vibrate to produce a very regular electric pulse of one hundred thousand or more cycles per second. The pulses pass through electronic microcircuits called dividing circuits, which keep dividing the pulse count, usually by ten, until the number is small enough to be used for display of time, day, and date on the dial.

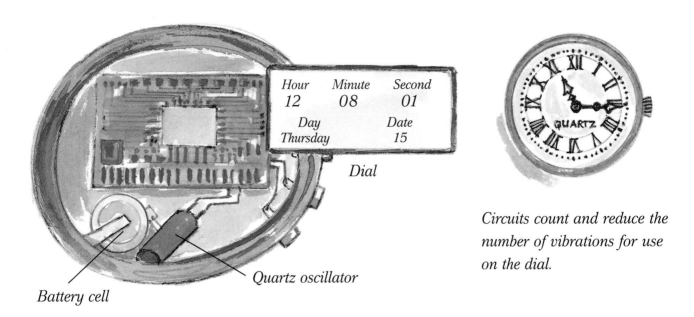

Hour	Minute	Second
12	08	01

Day	Date
Thursday	15

Dial

QUARTZ

Circuits count and reduce the number of vibrations for use on the dial.

Quartz oscillator

Battery cell

Atoms are sent through a long metallic resonator tube and energized to the required vibrations per second.

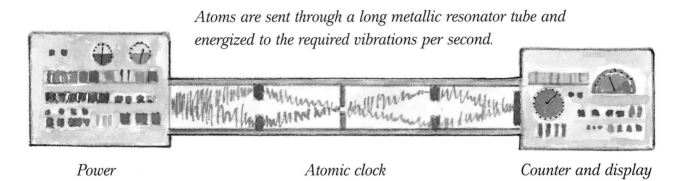

Power　　　　　*Atomic clock*　　　　　*Counter and display*

Atomic clocks, invented in 1952, use the vibrations of atoms to produce a pulse of billions of cycles per second. They have three primary parts: a power source; a resonator, to set the frequency, or number of pulse "ticks" per second; and a pulse counter/display.

These clocks are able to measure time in microseconds, millionths of a second; as well as nanoseconds, billionths of a second; and picoseconds, trillionths of a second. Way too fast for most of us to use!

One major timekeeping problem that arose in the fast-moving modern age was that of how to know what time it was in other locations.

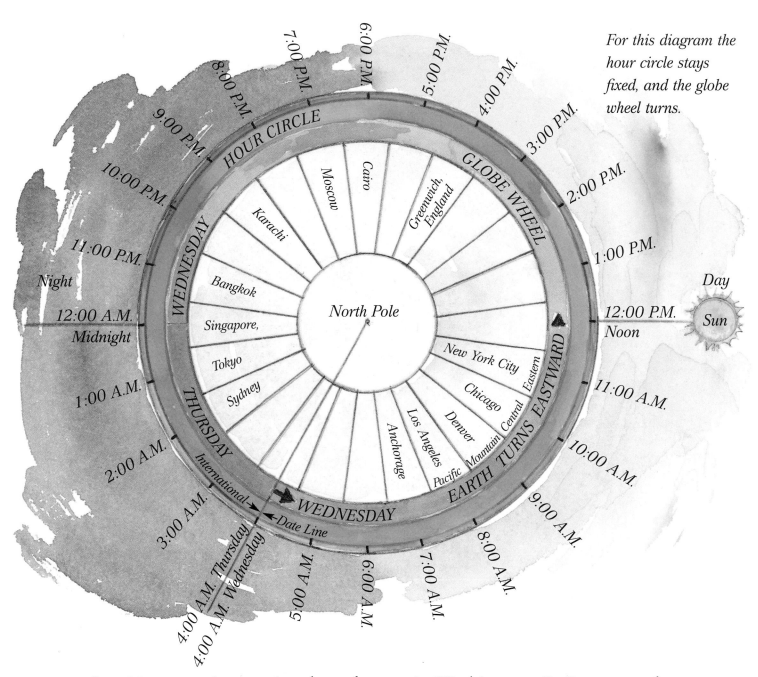

For this diagram the hour circle stays fixed, and the globe wheel turns.

In 1884, at an international conference in Washington, D.C., twenty-four world time zones were established, each having a one-hour time difference from the adjacent zone.

The continental United States uses four standard time zones: Pacific Time, (Rocky) Mountain Time, Central Time, and Eastern Time. Now someone in one part of the world can know what time it is in any other location in the world.

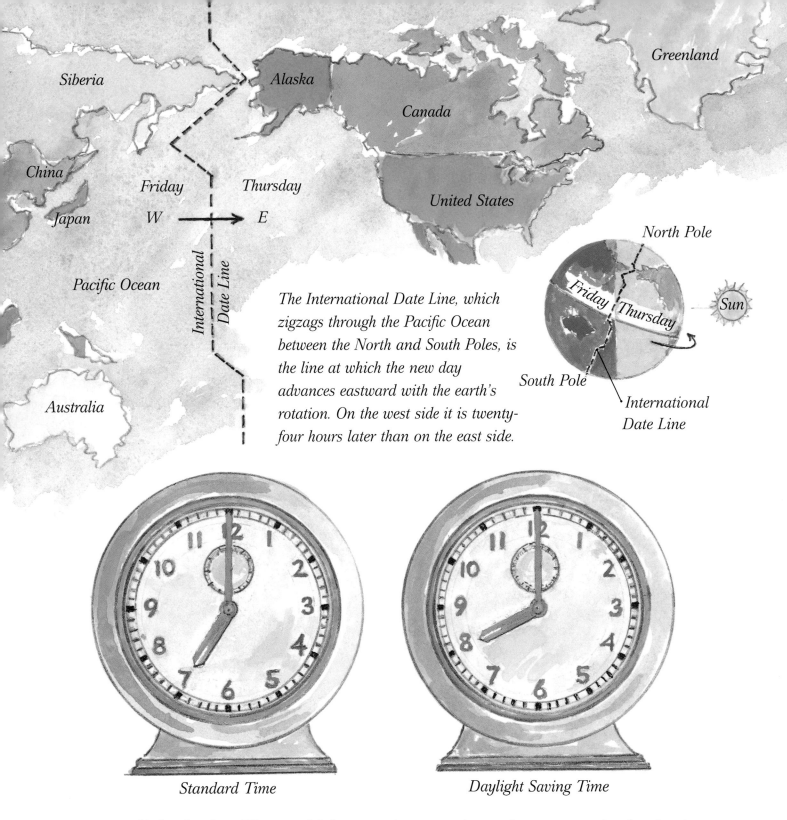

The International Date Line, which zigzags through the Pacific Ocean between the North and South Poles, is the line at which the new day advances eastward with the earth's rotation. On the west side it is twenty-four hours later than on the east side.

Standard Time

Daylight Saving Time

Daylight Saving Time, which came into use in various countries beginning in 1915 in order to save fuel and give people more time to enjoy the day, moves the clock ahead by one hour, allowing it to stay dark one hour later in the morning and light one hour later in the evening.

In the United States, Daylight Saving Time is used from the first Sunday in April until the last Sunday in October.

All this timekeeping precision, however, brings us back to the idea of "time" itself. Although people have always been able to use a clock of some sort to measure the time, when they took time to think about exactly what it was that they were measuring, there were many different ideas about that. Time has always been a topic as mysterious and difficult to grasp as it is important in our lives.

The Greeks, for example, thought that time was cyclical, that is, ever turning in a loop without beginning or end. In this view, everything gets recycled over and over again.

Saint Augustine, in the fifth century A.D., argued that time was not cyclical but that the world and time had one beginning and that time moves forward in a nonrepeating manner.

Albert Einstein changed our thinking about time in 1905 when he published his theory of relativity, tying together ideas about space, time, and motion. Today, modern science continues to consider many varied ideas, old and new, about time in order to better understand how time may play its part throughout the universe.

Thinking about time may leave us wondering ever more about its mystery. One thing we can say with some certainty, though, is that for as long as people are around, the last word on the topic of time hasn't been spoken.

I hope that reading this book has helped you to expand your view of time and to think about time in new ways—and that it's been a good use of your time.